When Inky waves her magic
A flying spell she'll send
To make a magic picnic ride
For Primrose – her best friend.

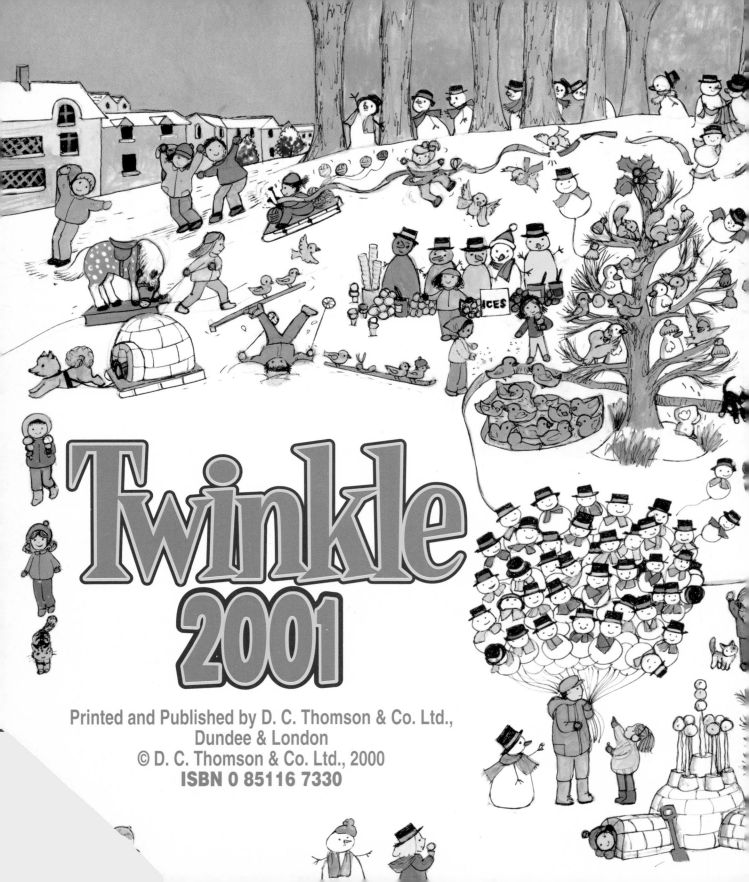

Twinkle
2001

Printed and Published by D. C. Thomson & Co. Ltd.,
Dundee & London
© D. C. Thomson & Co. Ltd., 2000
ISBN 0 85116 7330

Hello, everyone!
Welcome to Twinkle 2001 – 64 colourful pages of fun,
specially for you!
Look out for super stories – Santa's little helper,
Blackberry surprise and Mummy's new job, as well as
Twinkle favourites - Nurse Nancy, Silly Milly and the Blobs.
You'll find puzzles, games and things to do, too, all in the
brightest book around!

Have fun!
Love, TWINKLE

Nurse Nancy

Nancy is the nurse at the Dollies Hospital where her grandad is the doctor.

1 — One morning, Adam Curtis brought his teddy to the hospital. "Could you mend Bertie's ear while I'm on holiday?" he asked.

2 — Nancy agreed and was soon busy repairing the teddy bear's ear. When she had finished, she put on a bandage.

3 — "You'll have to stay here until Adam comes home," she told Bertie. After a few days, however, Nancy thought the little bear looked bored.

4 — Then Laura Healy arrived. Her teddy needed new stuffing. "That will take a while," said Nancy.

7 — While Laura and Bertie were at the Teddy Bears' Picnic, Nancy and her grandad carefully mended Timmy. He was soon looking better.

8 — Later, Nancy placed Timmy in a bed in the ward. She was sorry that the little bear had missed the picnic.

5 — Laura *was* sad. "I was going to take Timmy to a special Teddy Bears' Picnic this afternoon," she sighed.

6 — Nancy had an idea. "Why don't you take Bertie? He's well enough to go," she suggested. "Oh, *yes*!" agreed Laura happily.

9 — But when Laura returned with Bertie, she had a super surprise for Timmy and Nancy. She brought lots of leftover food so her bear and the other patients could enjoy their very own picnic in the garden. They all had a super time.

Dandy Lion

DANDY looked around and said,
"Dear me! The same old faces!
I'll send an invitation to
Some friends in far-off places!"

2 — Next day, Dandy woke to see
Rob Reindeer standing there!
And in his sledge was Silky Seal,
And Pete, the Polar Bear.

5 — George brought a yellow parasol
And set it in the shade,
While Mrs Hippo hurried up
With jugs of lemonade.

6 — Then Ella filled her trunk, to give
A most refreshing spray.
"Oh, thank you!" cried the visitors.
"This *is* a perfect day!"

3 — "How beautiful your jungle is!"
   The three friends cried with glee.
"So fresh and green! Why, in the snow,
   We never *see* a tree!"

4 — But soon, they had to sit and rest.
   "It's very hot!" they said.
"Don't worry now," cried Dandy Lion.
   "We'll make you cool, instead!"

7 — But when evening came at last,
   They sighed, "We mustn't stop!"
The pals fetched juicy fruit and filled
   The sledge right to the top.

8 —'Bye!" waved Silky, Pete and Rob.
   "It's been a lot of fun!"
And back to Snow Land they all sped,
   Beneath the setting sun.

fun to colour

Royal
Blue

Santa's Little Helper

ON Christmas Eve, Rusty, the little reindeer, was listening to Speedy, who was helping to pull Santa's sleigh.

"Santa gives each of the reindeer a lovely, silver bell," said Speedy.

Rusty nodded his head. He'd often wished he could have one, but he was too young to pull Santa's sleigh.

Rusty climbed into bed, but he seemed to be no sooner asleep than he felt one of Santa's elves shaking him.

"Rusty!" cried the elf. "Speedy's sleeping. I can't get him to wake up. Santa needs all the help he can get."

"*I* could help," offered Rusty.

2 — Soon, the little elf and Rusty were trotting through the snowy wood. At last, they came to a clearing.

Rusty saw little elves and fairies packing Santa's sleigh with gifts.

Rusty was led into a cosy, little house, where a cheerful man in red was ticking names off a long list.

"This is Rusty," said the elf." He's come in Speedy's place."

3 — Quickly, the elf explained about Speedy.

"Well, never mind," smiled Santa. "Rusty will be a great help. Show him what to do."

All evening, Rusty worked hard. Then Santa arrived.

Rusty watched as two large reindeer were harnessed to the sleigh.

"Come here, Rusty!" called Santa suddenly. "You've worked so well, you can help me deliver the Christmas presents."

Rusty climbed aboard and soon, they were setting off through the dark, starry night.

4 — Early next morning, when Santa had delivered the last present, he gave Rusty a present — a silver bell! Then Santa gave him Speedy's present.

Back at the reindeer home, Rusty told Speedy that Santa wasn't cross with him and gave him the gift.

"Maybe it's a bell like mine," said Rusty.

Speedy opened his present.

"It's a bell," he grinned. "But not like yours. It's a bell on an *alarm clock*!"

Rusty laughed, then he began to yawn.

"I must go to sleep now," he sighed.

And, with the little silver bell on his pillow, the little reindeer fell fast asleep!

The Blobs

... bright little blobs of paint who come out of a paintbox into the wonderful world of Paintbox Land.

PET'S PARLOUR

Puppy Purple and the surprise

One afternoon, King Royal Blue was taking his royal watchdog, Puppy Purple, for a walk in town. As they passed a dog grooming parlour, Puppy met his friend, Fifi, who had been inside for some beauty treatment.

Puppy wished he could visit the parlour, too.

"Sorry, Puppy. I can't afford it this week," said Royal Blue.

Back at the palace, Puppy Purple sat in front of the mirror.

"I look such a mess," he thought miserably.

Royal Blue felt sorry for his pup and he phoned Primrose Yellow to see if she could help.

The kindly Blob packed her best shampoo and brushes and set off for the palace straight away.

"You can have your own dog parlour right here," said Primrose setting to work.

In no time at all, Puppy was beautifully shampooed and groomed.

He did look smart.

"Ah, it's a dog life," sighed Puppy. "And I love it!"

Witch Winkle

Wendy Wilson has an unusual friend. A 300-year-old witch called Winkle.

1 — One day, the chums pitched a tent in Wendy's garden. "It'll be just like going camping," the little girl beamed, driving in the last peg.

2 — Just then, however, it started to rain. Wendy and Winkle crawled inside the tent.

"Oh, dear!" cried Winkle. "It's spoiled the day!"

Wendy's friends arrived and, because of the rain, they played indoors.

The boys and girls all wanted to do different things.

The shouting and laughter grew louder and louder until, at last, Wendy's mum could stand it no longer.

3 — "Oh, Winkle!" she groaned, holding her ears. "This noise is *terrible!*" Winkle nodded her head — she *had* to agree with Mum.

4 — "I'll fix this," Winkle decided and she chanted, *"Here's what I figure — make the tent bigger!"*

5 — In an instant, Wendy's tent grew to the size of a marquee. "Come on, everyone — there's lots of room in here now," she chuckled.

6 — Soon, grateful parents were bringing their children to Winkle's Play Den. And the happy witch was rewarded with a box of chocs!

PATCH A PICTURE

Some of the pictures in this happy scene are missing. Cut out the small pictures on the right and stick them in the correct places.

Elfie

Elfie is a tiny elf who lives secretly in Mary's doll's house. When he makes things happen, Mary thinks it's magic. Poochie, Mary's big dog, is Elfie's best friend.

1 — Elfie and Poochie watched as Mary's mummy strung festive lanterns between the trees. "I *love* Christmas!" cried Elfie excitedly.

4 — Then Elfie came across Mary's half-finished decoration and box of glittery beads. He began to thread on more beads.

5 — When he had finished, he pulled the threaded garland to the playroom and draped it around the doll's house.

2 — Later, Elfie spotted Mary threading some colourful beads to make decorations. "Leave that for now, Mary," called Mummy.

3 — When it grew dark, Mummy switched on the lanterns. Elfie was thrilled. "Aren't they pretty?" he gasped with delight.

6 — The beads sparkled like the *real* lanterns. Mary couldn't believe her eyes. "It's the magic!" she cried to her friends.

7 — Meanwhile, Elfie was smiling. "It's *magic*, all right, to have my very own Christmas lanterns," he sighed happily.

Silly Milly

She's always in a muddle

1 — One day, Mr Player, the director of the local drama club, asked Milly if she would like to help. Her first job was to change the scenery.

2 — But Milly put up a mountain scene instead of Sherwood Forest.

4 — At the dress rehearsal, Mr Player cried, *"Action!"* The atmosphere of the play was spoiled, however, when Milly appeared on stage.

5 — Just then, someone opened a trap-door. *"Aagh!"* yelled Milly.

3 — After a few more mistakes, Milly was asked to work the stage lights. The silly miss couldn't control the spotlight, though, and the beam bounced *everywhere,* missing the actors completely.

6 — She landed on a mattress underneath the stage. *"Help!* I can't do *anything* down here," complained Milly. "That's the idea," laughed one of the actors. "Now we can get on with our play!"

Cuddles and Co.

Cuddles, the dog, and cats, Midge and Tiny, all live at Nadia's house. Nadia loves her pets and has lots of fun with them.

1 — One afternoon, the pets were bored playing in the garden. "Let's see what Nadia's up to," suggested Cuddles to his chums.

2 — Nadia's mummy was about to throw out some old magazines. Nadia asked if she could have them. "I want to cut out some of the pictures," she explained.

3 — Inside the house, Nadia's pets watched curiously as she carefully cut the pictures from the magazine. "I wonder what Nadia's going to do with these?" purred Tiny the kitten.

4 — Some time later, Nadia held up a large sheet of cardboard with all the pictures stuck on to it. "How do you like my super new fashion poster?" she smiled.

5 — Nadia went upstairs to put the poster on her bedroom wall. When she returned, Midge was trying to turn a page with her paw.

6 — Nadia turned the page for Midge and found that it was all about *cats!* "Oh, I see," laughed the little girl. "You want me to make a poster for *you!*" "Miaow!" agreed Midge.

7 — "What do you think?" asked Nadia when the cat poster was finished. Midge and Tiny *were* pleased — especially when Nadia hung it up on the wall beside their basket!

Cut-out Fun

Carefully cut out the figures of Cuddles and his chums. Then fold back the tabs to make them stand.

Blackberry Surprise

LUCY lived in a tiny cottage next to Tangle Wood. There were lots of blackberries growing at the bottom of Lucy's garden. One day, Mummy decided to make a blackberry pie.

"Take your basket, Lucy," said her mummy, "and fetch me some large, juicy blackberries."

Soon, Lucy was wriggling past the thorns and creepers of the blackberry bushes to get the juiciest berries.

"Mmm!" she sighed, tasting another berry. "I *love* blackberries!"

Soon, the basket was almost full. Tired Lucy let out a geat yawn.

"Ooh!" she said sleepily. "I think I'll have to go home now."

2 — Lucy was about to set off up the path, when she spotted the biggest berries she had ever seen.

But, no matter how hard she tried, Lucy *couldn't* pull any berries from the bush.

Lucy tugged at the berries again, but nothing happened.

Lucy couldn't bring herself to leave the fruit, however.

"I'll give it one more try," she decided.

So, Lucy pulled with all her might. At last, a berry came away from the bush — but so did something else!

3 — "Hoi!" shouted a little voice. "What do you think you're doing?"

Lucy *did* get a surprise for, perched on top of the berries in her basket, was a little elf!

"Who are you?" asked Lucy.

"I'm Bertie," replied the tiny creature. "I made some magic so that you couldn't pull the berries from the bush."

"So I ended up with *you* in the basket instead," said Lucy laughing.

4 — "Do you live in Tangle Wood?" asked Lucy.

"Oh, yes!" said Bertie.

Bertie led Lucy along the path to a pretty little house in the trunk of a tree.

"I'd invite you in," he chuckled, "but you're too big."

Then Lucy noticed that it was getting dark and, waving goodbye to her new friend, she hurried home.

Soon, the smell of blackberries and pastry filled the kitchen as Mummy lifted a tasty pie from the oven. Lucy had used some leftover berries to bake two small pies and they were ready, too!

"One for me," thought Lucy with a smile, "and one to give Bertie when I visit him tomorrow."

I SPY

It's Christmas party time at the Dollies Hospital. Join in the fun with Nancy and Colin by playing this super I Spy game.
Roll the dice to see who goes first then set off around the board. As each player lands on a square, they must spy something in the picture beginning with the letter in that square. If they can't find something, they're out! No object can be spied twice. Keep going until one person is left — the winner!

ONE night when we were fast asleep,
  The snow fell thick and fast.
And Daddy, to surprise us, built
  A snowman on the grass.

2 — Of course, Ben wanted to go out
  And fetched his winter clothes.
But Mummy said, "They're much too small,
  You've grown too big for those."

My Baby Brother

3 — So Benny wore his other gloves,
  Warm coat and hat and scarf.
But he looked at his out-grown things
  And then began to laugh.

4 — "I'll build a boy all made of snow
  To wear these clothes," he said.
"He'll keep the snowman company
  When we have gone to bed."

5 — Next morning, I woke up young Ben,
"Don't laze around," I said.
"Get dressed! It's time to have some fun.
Come on, you sleepy head!"

6 — So, Ben threw off his cosy quilt
And scrambled from his bed.
"Perhaps the snow has gone," he sighed,
"And rain has come instead."

7 — But outside, to our great delight,
Our snow chums were still there,
And little flakes of sparkling snow
Swirled softly in the air.

8 — We took our sledge on to the hill
A super place to play.
"Oh, snowy days are just the *best!*"
I heard my brother say.

PUZZLE TIME

Lotti the cave girl has found a huge egg. She doesn't know who it belongs to.

A cute baby dinosaur has hatched from the egg. Can you find six differences between these pictures of the baby?

Lotti decides to help the dinosaur find its mummy. They cross the Crocosaurus River *very* carefully. Which two stepping stones are exactly alike?

Safely on the other side, Lotti meets a strange creature. Join the dots to see if it's the dino's mummy.

Lotti discovers a cave with writing on the wall. Rearrange the letters to see what it says.

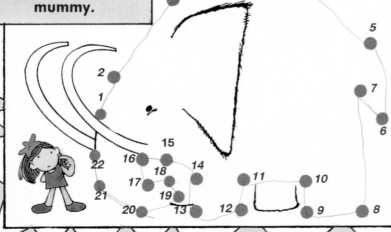

Happy Lotti has returned the baby dinosaur to its mummy in Dinosaur Land. Fill in the dotted areas if you want to see these dinosaurs. How many can you count?

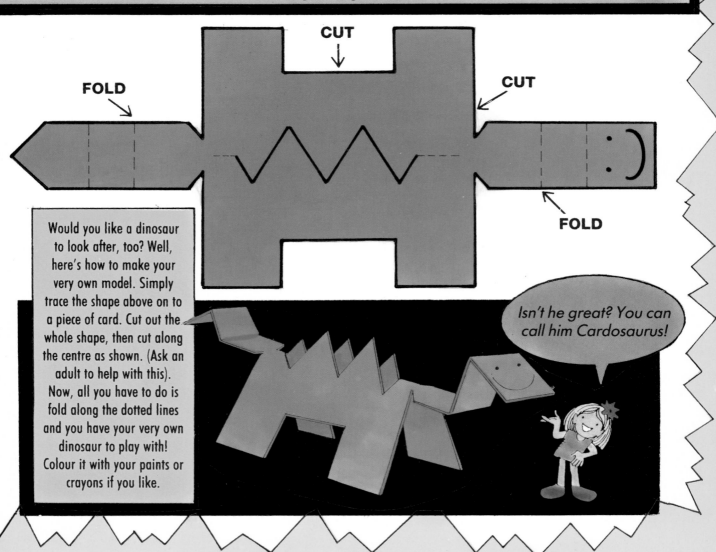

Would you like a dinosaur to look after, too? Well, here's how to make your very own model. Simply trace the shape above on to a piece of card. Cut out the whole shape, then cut along the centre as shown. (Ask an adult to help with this). Now, all you have to do is fold along the dotted lines and you have your very own dinosaur to play with! Colour it with your paints or crayons if you like.

Garden Search

Look at the small pictures around the page and see if you can find them in the big scene.

Nurse Nancy

1 — Nurse Nancy had an unusual patient. It was a reindeer with a broken antler. Nancy bandaged the antler.

4 — "I know how to mend Rudi," grinned Nancy later. So Grandad set to work while Nancy put up decorations.

2 — But when Nancy's grandad took off the bandage, Rudi's antler snapped. "It's not going to mend," said Grandad.

3 — Then, when shopping for decorations, Nancy saw two sparkling branches which she thought would be very useful.

5 — Next day, there was a special patients' Christmas party! When everyone sang "Jingle Bells", not only did *Santa* appear, *Rudi* did, too, with bright, new antlers and lots of gifts!

A POOL FOR POPPY

POPPY the duck lives on Mill Farm. One day, the farm children, Daniel and Lizzy, visited Poppy's ducklings.

2 — Later, Poppy decided to take her babies for a swim. But grumpy Celia swan hissed, "Go away!"

3 — Then Lizzy had an idea. She asked Daddy to fill the paddling pool for Poppy and the ducklings. Soon, they were having a lovely swim. Poppy *was* pleased to have her very *own* pool!

Mummy's New Job

SOPHIE'S mummy had invited her friend, Helene, over for coffee one morning.

Sophie was pouring pretend cups of tea for her teddies and her favourite doll, Emma, while Mummy and Helene chatted.

"When do you start your new job?" Helene asked Mummy.

"Tomorrow," Mummy replied.

"Oh, no," thought Sophie. "If Mummy has a job, who will look after *me*?"

Sophie's best friend, Leigh-Anne, was looked after by a childminder while her mummy was out to work.

"Maybe *I'll* go to a childminder," thought Sophie.

2 — Next morning, Sophie waved to her daddy as he left for work.

"When will Mummy go to work?" Sophie wondered.

Mummy was washing the breakfast things and didn't seem to be in any hurry.

"Mummy's new job could be at night when I'm in bed," Sophie decided. "Before I was born, she used to be a nurse in the hospital. Some nurses work during the night."

"Let's tidy up your bedroom now, Sophie," said Mummy later. "And when we've done that, I think we'll move some of your toys into the spare room."

3 — A little later, there was a knock at the door.

"Come and meet Lee," cried Mummy. "He'll be coming here every day while his parents go to work."

"So that's Mummy's new job — a *childminder!*" thought Sophie. "She'll be working at home."

Sophie and Lee had lots of fun playing with the toys, painting pictures and listening to Mummy reading stories from books.

Then a few week's later, there was lots more fun when Mummy became Leigh-Anne's childminder, too. This pleased Sophie very much.

"I *do* like your new job, Mummy!" said the little girl with a grin.

Dandy Lion

ON Christmas Eve, the snow lay thick around Dandy Lion's house. "Hooray!" he roared. "Now for some fun!"

Dandy hurried outside. He began to roll a snowball along the ground. Some jungle birds flew down to watch as it grew bigger and bigger.

The birds looked cold, huddled together on the branch. Dandy had an idea! "I'll turn this snowball into a *foodball* for the birds," he thought.

Dandy fetched currants, cherries, nuts and raisins and stuck them all over the snowball. Then he put a sprig of holly on top. It looked just like a *huge* Christmas pudding.

"Oh, thanks!" chirped the hungry birds. "This is a real Christmas *tweet!*"

Sara and Sam

ONE rainy day, Sara and Sam Bright visited the zoo with their mummy. Unfortunately, Sara and Sam hardly saw any of the animals. They didn't like getting wet so they stayed inside their shelters.

The children *were* disappointed and returned home in the car.

"It's not fair," grumbled Sam. "I *hate* the rain!"

Sara and Sam had just arrived back when the sun started to shine.

"We can't go back to the zoo," said Mummy. "It costs too much to go twice in the same day."

Sara had a fun idea, however. She arranged all their cuddly toy animals around the garden and invited their friends over to see the *toy* zoo.

"Write down how many animals you can spot?" said Sara handing out pieces of paper.

Answers
Bear
Elephant
Monkey
Horse
Snake
Tortoise
Lion
Giraffe

How many cuddly toy animals can you spot? The answers are at the side of this picture.

The Blobs

... bright little blobs of paint who come out of a paintbox into the wonderful world of Paintbox Land.

Primrose Yellow's bright idea

Primrose Yellow and her friend, Poppy Red, were shopping one morning.

"These are just what I need," said Primrose as she passed a display of sunglasses.

"Are you going on holiday?" asked Poppy Red.

"No. They're not for the sun. They're for a special visit this afternoon," laughed Primrose mysteriously.

Primrose tried on lots of pairs of sunglasses – red, blue, green, all colours and styles.

"I think *this* pair suits me best," she said, after trying on a pretty pink pair.

Poppy thought so, too.

And so, that afternoon, Primrose set out wearing her new sunglasses.

She really needed them, because she was visiting a Blobs chum who has the most *colourful* house in Paintbox Land. The walls are all the colours of the rainbow. It's so *bright* – it *dazzles* the sun!

"My new sunglasses are perfect for having tea with Rainbow Blob," grinned Primrose happily.

To play this super winter sports game,
all you need is a dice and counters. Roll the dice
to see who starts. Follow the instructions and have fun,
skiing, climbing or riding up and down the mountains.
First to the finish wins.

WINTER

39
40
41
42
43

Jump back to 36.

38
37
36
35

Whee! Ski back down to 18.

19
21
22

20

Hold on! You're going on a ride to 43.

18
17
16
14

Take a sleigh ride back to start.

15

START

1
2
3

Fairy Fay

1 — One autumn night, Duncan Dormouse broke his alarm clock. "I'm hibernating soon. I'll never waken up without my alarm!" he cried.

2 — Fairy Fay visited Duncan the next day. When he told her about the clock, she offered to fetch a new one for her friend.

3 — But the clockmaker had sold all his clocks. "There's been a rush on them," he told Fay. "The squirrels and hedgehogs bought them."

4 — Fay decided to waken Duncan herself. Soon, the dormouse was asleep in his bed where he would remain until April.

5 — The cold winter days passed. On very chilly mornings, Fay did some "hibernating" too — lying in her cosy bed a little bit longer.

6 — Then one morning, a little robin fluttered on to the end of her bed. "*Wake up*! *Wake up*!" he chirped. "Spring is here!"

7 — Fay hurried to look at her calendar. "It's *April*!" she cried. "I waken Duncan today."

8 — And later, Fay brought her friend breakfast in bed. "Wakey, wakey," she called softly. "What a lovely alarm call," sighed Duncan happily.

FUN TO COLOUR

Rosie and Rags

1 — One day, Rosie decided to wash some of her clothes. Rags watched her curiously.

2 — Rosie turned the tap on *full*, splashing herself and Rags with the water.

3 — Then she added the soap powder. "This looks like fun," thought Rags.

4 — Rags jumped up beside Rosie tipping more powder in the sink.

5 — Suddenly, frothy bubbles overflowed from the sink. Rosie and Rags loved them.

6 — "What a mess!" gasped Mum. "I think *I'll* do the washing!"

7 — Mum sent Rosie and Rags out to play with Jamie next door. They had great fun blowing *lots* and *lots* of bubbles!

Patch

1 — One day, Paula Perkins was sewing a picture for her mum. Patch, her kitten, wanted to help. "Sorry, Patch, you'll get my wool in a mess," said Paula with a smile. "Off you go."

2 — Patch wasn't pleased so he went off and sulked behind a bush. Paula didn't notice, however, because she was working hard. Soon, she needed a cool drink.

3 — While Paula was enjoying her drink, a robin flew down on to the lawn. The little bird wasn't afraid of Patch at all as the curious kitten padded towards it.

4 — When Paula came back, her red wool was missing. "Did you take my wool, naughty Patch?" she asked.

5 — Poor Patch! But before he could even miaow, Mummy cried, "Look at that cheeky robin!"

6 — "It's taking your wool for its nest," explained Mummy. "And I blamed *Patch!*" laughed Paula. Patch didn't mind, though, and lay happily in Paula's arms purring *very* loudly.

1 — Polly Penguin lives in Snowland with her chums. One morning, Peter Polar Bear arrived at Polly's house with his toy train. It *was* smart.

2 — "Come and have a ride in it, Polly," said Peter excitedly. So, Polly climbed in the coal truck and Peter set off. They headed for the supermarket.

3 — Outside the shop, the chums found the mummy polar bears laden with bags. "Oh, dear, we've bought too much. We can't push our babies home with our hands full," they said.

4 — Polly had an idea to help. She and Peter set to work and tied all the babies' prams together with pieces of rope. "Nearly ready," cried the clever little penguin cheerfully.

5 — Then they tied the prams carefully to the back of Peter's train. "Hold on tight, everyone," said Polly, as Peter gave a *toot* on the whistle.

6 — Soon the train, with the prams in tow, was chugging through the snow. "Well done," said the grateful Mums. The babies had great fun, too.

Now all aboard the Blobsea bus,
The Blobs chums shout – "Hooray!"
Look! Rainbow Blob's behind the wheel,
To chase the clouds away!

blobsea

to the seaside